Did you know?

A timeline shows you the order that t~~
happened in the past. On the tim~
page 30, the dates that were ~
at the top. The dates get close.
as you read down the timeline.

Think and remember

Which sports and games do you like to
play? How many different sports can you
think of? Now try and remember as many
different board games as possible.

Mini's Top Spot

Can you find the index in this book?

Index

backgammon	22
basketball	12
chess	25
football	8–9

Is your favourite sport or game included in the book?

Before you read

Word alert

- Read the words.

  they're   that's   can't   aren't

- These words all have apostrophes for contraction: where two words are shortened and joined to make one word. The apostrophe shows where a letter or letters have been missed out.

- Which words have been contracted to make these words?

  it's   don't   wasn't   you've

- Look out for other words with apostrophes for contraction when you are reading.

What does it mean?

sensational – very exciting

strategy – a plan of action designed to reach a long-term goal

Time to find out …

As you read, use the Expert Tip **Think and remember** to help you answer this question:

- *How do we know about the sports and games people played in the past?*

Ancient sports

Today, we play sport at school, with friends and in competitions – but have you ever wondered how long ago humans started playing sport? We aren't exactly sure, but old artwork suggests it could have been many thousands of years ago.

These cave paintings were made between 6000 and 9000 years ago. Some of the figures look like they're swimming. Could they be racing?

swimming figure

Sporting life

Sport was an important part of life in many ancient **civilizations**. People showed off their fighting skills in wrestling and boxing matches. Historians think that some sports, like bull leaping, could have been part of religious events.

This is a section of a wall painting in Crete from about 1550 BC. Imagine leaping over this bull's horns!

Ancient Rome's rulers used sport to show off their power. They built grand **stadiums** that could fit thousands of people inside.

A favourite Roman sport was chariot racing. Vast crowds of **spectators** gathered to watch.

Lots of chariots raced at a time. Each chariot had four horses so the race must have been sensational and dangerous!

Cuju

Today's game of football is similar to a game played in China over 2200 years ago. Kickball or 'cuju' (*say* tsoo-joo) was played with a ball called a 'ju'. The ju was leather on the outside and stuffed with feathers. 'Cuju' means 'to kick the ball with the foot'.

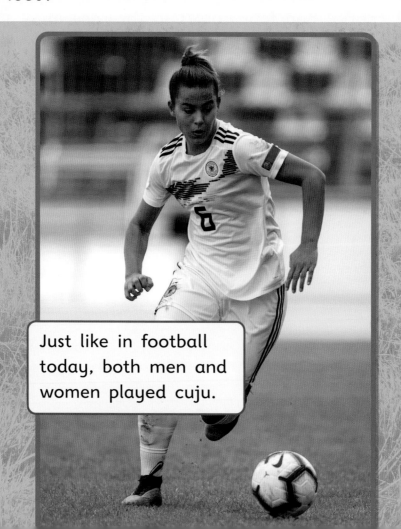

Just like in football today, both men and women played cuju.

Cuju's rules changed over time but they were a bit like the rules of football. The main aim was to kick the ball through a 'goal' using only the feet or the head. Players on opposing teams wore different colours. The team that scored the most goals won.

Cuju was a game played to entertain important people. Even **emperors** played it!

Kemari

In the old Japanese ballgame of kemari, players try to keep a ball in the air while passing it to each other. Players are judged by their speed and skill.

Kemari is still played today at special events.

Samurai warriors played kemari in their spare time to show off their impressive skills. Samurai warriors were Japanese soldiers. They were expert swordsmen.

Do you think you could keep a ball up in the air while dressed in a hat and flowing robes? That's what the **noblemen** of Japan did to entertain their rulers.

Ulama

Where did the ideas for volleyball and basketball come from? Could they have come from an old Mayan ballgame called ulama (*say oo-lar-ma*)? Ulama was played on a court with a rubber ball and rings.

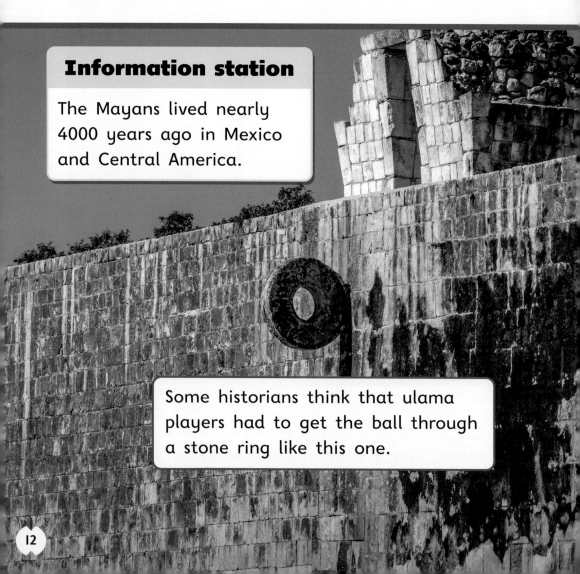

Information station

The Mayans lived nearly 4000 years ago in Mexico and Central America.

Some historians think that ulama players had to get the ball through a stone ring like this one.

Players had to keep the ball in motion by using their hips, knees and elbows. They bounced it off the walls to their teammates. It must have been a very tricky game!

The largest ulama court ever found is in Mexico.

Take action

Can you pass a ball or balloon between you and your friends without it touching the floor?

The Olympic Games

What do you think it would feel like to represent your nation in the Olympic or Paralympic Games? Would you like to be part of a national team?

The very first Olympic Games were held about 2800 years ago in Olympia, Greece.

About 40 000 spectators filled these slopes around the original running track.

The first Olympic Games only had one event: a running race known as the 'stade'. It was called this because the track was one stade long. A stade was a Greek unit of measurement of about 180 to 200 metres.

The modern word 'stadium' comes from 'stade'.

Can you imagine arriving at the competition through this tunnel to the roar of a huge crowd?

Additional events

The Ancient Greeks held the Olympic Games every four years until AD 393. They added more events to the competition, including:

- throwing
- jumping
- chariot racing
- pankration.

Pankration was a dangerous fighting sport. The Greeks believe Theseus started the sport after he beat the minotaur. It's still played today in some places, but with different rules.

A new competition

In 1896, a Frenchman decided to restart the Olympic Games. Fourteen nations competed in the first modern Olympic Games in Greece.

The start of the men's 100 m race in 1896 looked very different to today's races.

Take action

Can you invent your own competition? What events would you include?

Ancient games

Children have enjoyed playground games like tag for many years, probably even for thousands of years. We can't be sure because we don't always have **evidence** to prove it.

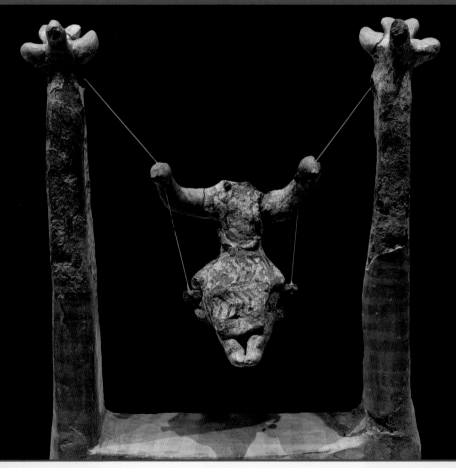

This clay model was made thousands of years ago. It tells us that the Ancient Greeks had swings.

Hopscotch

Some historians think Ancient Roman soldiers played a kind of hopscotch as part of their workouts. They put on all of their armour and hopped up and down a grid scratched into the ground.

Can you imagine playing hopscotch while wearing heavy metal armour? It must have been very difficult!

Board games

How many kinds of board games can you think of? Some of today's popular games are inventions from thousands of years ago. Versions of these games were played by ancient civilizations in Africa, Western Asia and Southern Asia.

'Snakes and ladders' was invented in India, but historians aren't sure exactly when. It could have been 800 years ago or over 2000 years ago.

The earliest kinds of board games are called 'mancala'. 'Mancala' comes from the Arabic word meaning 'to move'. These games involved actions similar to planting seeds, such as counting out and carefully placing counters.

small stones used as 'seeds'

This early board game was scratched into a stone slab about 3500 years ago in Kenya.

Senet

In a 'strategy game' you place your game pieces to create puzzles for your **opponent** to **overcome**. Senet is an **Ancient Egyptian** strategy board game similar to today's backgammon. 'Senet' means 'passing'.

modern backgammon board

King Tutankhamun was buried with five sets of the game senet.

In senet, players had to get their pieces across the board. They threw sticks to decide how to move their pieces. A player could block another player or force them to go back. This was all part of the strategy of the game.

A painting on the wall of Queen Nefertari's tomb shows her playing senet.

Noughts and crosses

Have you ever played the strategy game 'noughts and crosses'? One player is 'noughts' and the other 'crosses'. They take turns to draw a 0 or X in a nine-square grid, until someone gets three in a row.

Noughts win!

Take action

Have a go at playing noughts and crosses with a friend.

The Ancient Romans played a version named 'terni lapilli', which means 'three little stones'.

Chess

A strategy game similar to chess started in India about 1500 years ago. Its popularity spread worldwide. Old chess pieces have been found in Central Asia, China, Europe, Pakistan and Russia.

These chess pieces are about 800 years old and were found in Scotland.

Go

The strategy board game Go is 4000 years old. It was invented in China, where it is called 'weiqi' (*say* way-chee). It's also popular in Japan, where it is called 'igo'. At one point, Japan had four special Go schools. At these schools, Go wasn't just entertainment, but a sport that needed a lot of skill.

Go was a popular **pastime** for ladies in the palace courtyards in China.

Go is a game for two players. Players use stones called 'go-ishi' on a board called a 'goban'. The aim of the game is to win areas of the board by making boundaries with the stones.

The rules of Go are so simple that different generations can enjoy playing the game together.

Three men's morris

Board games have been enjoyed for thousands of years. Now that you've learned all about them, follow these instructions to make a game from Ancient Rome to play yourself.

Instructions

1. Use a ruler to draw a square on a piece of paper.
2. Draw a line across the square.
3. Draw another line down through the square.
4. Draw two lines from corner to corner.
5. Add a dot every time two or more lines touch.
6. Make six counters: three in one colour and three in a different colour. You are ready to play!

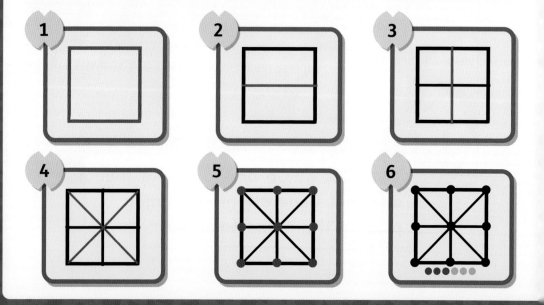

How to play

Each player has three counters, or 'men'. You win by having placed three counters down on three dots that are next to each other and joined by a straight line.

You can put your first counter anywhere. Take it in turns to place your counters. Continue taking turns to move one counter to any empty dot until someone wins.

You can make the game harder by changing the design of the board.

Now you're playing a game from history!

Timeline

(approximate dates)

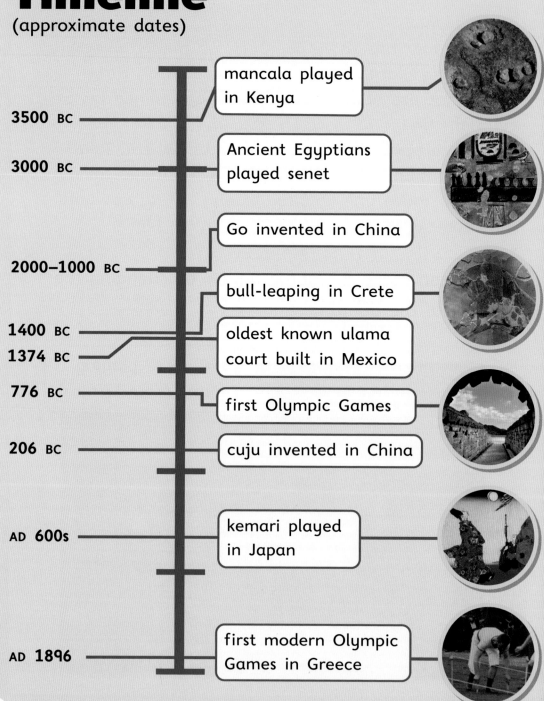

3500 BC — mancala played in Kenya

3000 BC — Ancient Egyptians played senet

Go invented in China

2000–1000 BC —

bull-leaping in Crete

1400 BC —
1374 BC — oldest known ulama court built in Mexico

776 BC — first Olympic Games

206 BC — cuju invented in China

AD 600s — kemari played in Japan

AD 1896 — first modern Olympic Games in Greece

Glossary

Ancient Egyptians	people who lived along the river Nile in north Africa between about 3000 BC and 30 BC
Ancient Rome	the civilization controlled by the city of Rome that lasted from the 8th century BC to the 5th century AD
civilization	human society
emperor	someone who rules an empire (a group of countries that are controlled together)
evidence	objects, writing or art that prove something to be true
nobleman	a man from a powerful, high-ranking family
opponent	a person who competes against someone else in a contest or game
overcome	to overpower or defeat (an opponent)
pastime	an activity that is carried out for fun
spectator	a person who watches an event or a show
stadium	a large sports ground

Index

31

Now you have read ...

Ancient Sports and Games

 Stop and check it makes sense – take action

Each of these ancient sports and games has a link to something that we play today. Match up the pairs.

terni lapilli

cuju

ulama

senet

backgammon

basketball

football

noughts and crosses

 Think and remember

How do we know about ancient sports and games? Think about the ways historians found out about the sports and games in this book.

32